MW00635634

Heather Torgenrud

Pick-Up Bandweaving Designs

288 Charts for 13 Pattern Ends

— AND —

Techniques for Arranging Color

SCHIFFER
CRAFT

4880 Lower Valley Road • Atglen, PA 19310

Other Schiffer Craft Books by the Author:

Norwegian Pick-Up Bandweaving, ISBN 978-0-7643-4751-1

Other Schiffer Craft Books on Related Subjects:

Easy Weaving with Supplemental Warps: Overshot, Velvet, Shibori, and More, Deb Essen, ISBN 978-0-7643-6470-9

Nordic Hands: 25 Fiber Craft Projects to Discover Scandinavian Culture, Anita Osterhaug, ISBN 978-0-7643-6691-8

Weaving Patterned Bands: How to Create and Design with 5, 7, and 9 Pattern Threads, Susan J. Foulkes, ISBN 978-0-7643-5550-9

Copyright © 2024 by Heather Torgenrud

Library of Congress Control Number: 2024931549

All rights reserved. No part of this work may be reproduced or used in any form or by any means—graphic, electronic, or mechanical, including photocopying or information storage and retrieval systems—without written permission from the publisher.

The scanning, uploading, and distribution of this book or any part thereof via the Internet or any other means without the permission of the publisher is illegal and punishable by law. Please purchase only authorized editions and do not participate in or encourage the electronic piracy of copyrighted materials.

"Schiffer Craft" and the crane logo are registered trademarks of Schiffer Publishing, Ltd.

Designed by Heather Torgenrud
Cover design by Ashley Millhouse
Charts, woven samples, and photographs by Heather Torgenrud
Type set in Mr. Eaves and Adobe Garamond Pro

ISBN: 978-0-7643-6813-4
Printed in China

Published by Schiffer Craft
An imprint of Schiffer Publishing, Ltd.
4880 Lower Valley Road
Atglen, PA 19310
Phone: (610) 593-1777; Fax: (610) 593-2002
Email: Info@schifferbooks.com
Web: www.schifferbooks.com

For our complete selection of fine books on this and related subjects, please visit our website at www.schifferbooks.com. You may also write for a free catalog.

Schiffer Publishing's titles are available at special discounts for bulk purchases for sales promotions or premiums. Special editions, including personalized covers, corporate imprints, and excerpts, can be created in large quantities for special needs. For more information, contact the publisher.

We are always looking for people to write books on new and related subjects. If you have an idea for a book, please contact us at proposals@schifferbooks.com.

In loving memory of my husband, Don Torgenrud

When we were first together, I was learning to weave on a Lily Mills table loom. One day Don said that he'd seen a little bandweaving loom for sale, and he asked if that was something I'd like. "No thanks," I replied. "I'm not at all interested in weaving bands." The following week he gave me the loom as a gift. The year was 1972.

*A basket of pick-up bands!
These tiny textiles pack a punch—with
patterns based on dynamic diagonal lines and
lots of color and texture.*

Fig. 1: Here's a peek at some of the samples we'll look at in Part 2. *From left to right and top to bottom*, these are woven from Chart Nos. 277, 136, 126, 105, 54, 30, 33, 61, 82, 108, 186, 98, 67, 147, 178, 134, 103, 114, 200, 72, 277, 119, 89, 17, 36, 129, 284, 45, 161–162, 90, 106, 92, 191, 141, 40, 166.

Contents

Introduction

Fig. 2: Light Rust with Magenta on Natural, Charts 145 and 199.

If you know how to weave pick-up bands and are looking for new design ideas, you've come to the right place.

My first book, *Norwegian Pick-Up Bandweaving*, documented bands in traditional patterns and colors from the Vesterheim Norwegian-American Museum collection and told the story of their place in the old Norwegian farm society. The book you now hold in your hands is different. With 288 pattern charts and an in-depth look at ways to arrange color in pick-up bands, it illustrates how both pattern and color can be varied creatively while still staying in touch with the essence of this heritage craft. If you're interested in how I developed this collection of charts, see page 89 for a description of my design process.

In Part 1, all 288 charts are for 13 pattern ends. Thirteen is my favorite number of ends to work with—enough so I don't run out of pattern ideas yet easy to keep track of as I weave. You can combine any of these patterns in the same band, and you'll find ideas for charting transitions between them on page 86.

The charts are in neutral gray so you can more easily imagine them in your own colors. But Part 2 is all about ways to arrange color in pick-up bands, with 68 woven samples that illustrate accents, tone-on-tone combinations, two background colors, and more.

The charts are for a weave structure that is part of the folk traditions in many countries, and there's no universal name for it. In *Norwegian Pick-Up Bandweaving*, I followed the lead of the classic Swedish book *Band* (Trotzig and Axelsson 1972) and called it Type 2 pick-up, but many weavers refer to it as Baltic style.

Whatever you call it, it's a beautiful technique with intricate designs and a unique texture. You can see its characteristic appearance in the band in fig. 2—raised motifs in pattern color, a receding basketweave texture in background color, geometric patterns based on intersecting diagonal lines, and a naturally pleasing visual balance between light and dark. On the reverse, the pattern and background change places for an equally appealing look.

You'll notice that I refer to one pass of the weft as a *shot* rather than a *pick,* and that I call the underlying woven structure *tabby* rather than *plain weave.* These choices are explained in the glossary.

For me, the joy of weaving pick-up bands springs not only from the strong appeal of the patterns, colors, and textures, but also from the rhythm of the weaving process itself. This rhythm develops not only because I'm working in a consistent way shot after shot, but also because there is an inherent rhythm in the threading and in the patterns that grow out of that threading. I hope that you enjoy weaving these patterns as much as I do and that you find lots of ideas in these pages to inspire your creativity and increase your enjoyment of this heritage craft.

Part 1

Charts

Charts

Fig. 3: Here Charts 189–192 illustrate four ways to segue between tabby and pick-up at the ends of a band.

This section of the book contains 288 numbered charts. Following the charts are two sidebars—one showing ways to transition between different patterns and one describing my design process. If you'd like to know which charts were used for the woven samples in this book, you'll find a key on page 119. Since you already know how to weave pick-up, the warp drafts and pattern charts will be familiar to you, but here is a brief summary:

About the Warp Drafts

- For the charts in this book, the warp must contain 13 pattern ends.
- Pattern ends are always separated by two background ends.
- The pattern yarn is thicker than the background yarn and weft, or it can be the same but doubled.
- The warp specifications for my woven samples are on page 120.

About the Pattern Charts

- One vertical column represents one pattern end. One horizontal row represents the position of the pattern ends in relation to one shot of weft.
- A darkened square means that the pattern end is visible on the face (above the weft) on that shot. A blank square means that the pattern end is visible on the reverse (below the weft) on that shot.
- Patterns are drawn on a square grid but appear more elongated when woven.
- The first motif must begin on the correct shed so that the pattern will be positioned correctly in relation to the staggered threading and the underlying weave structure.

Transitions between Tabby and Pick-Up

There are various ways to transition between tabby and pick-up at the beginning and end of a band, so this isn't shown on the charts. Four options are illustrated in fig. 3. I like the first or leftmost example because it shows the pick-up growing naturally out of the tabby flecks. The third and fourth options are good alternatives for a more planned look. For short samples, I often use the second option.

Weaving Methods

How you view the chart and apply it to your work depends on how you weave. When I weave on the band heddle or inkle loom, I use the positions of the pattern ends on each shed as prompts, and I make the pick-ups and push-downs with my fingers. For this method, I don't isolate horizontal rows on the chart, since I'm looking at how the pattern ends relate to one another along diagonal lines and within the pattern as a whole. I place the chart on an inexpensive music stand next to me and glance at it as needed. When I weave on the pattern heddle, I select the floating pattern ends on each shed with a pointed shuttle and find it helpful to periodically focus on one horizontal row while still keeping the whole chart in perspective. For this method, I place the chart on a chair or bench next to me and use a translucent reading aid as needed (see fig. 4).

Fig. 4: With some weaving methods, it can be helpful to isolate a horizontal row while still keeping the whole chart in perspective. A translucent reading aid is a handy tool for this, and removable highlighter tape is another option. If you're weaving from a book, you can hold it open with a book weight or clip, but consider copying the chart onto graph paper instead. Sketching in the floats and flecks is a good way to familiarize yourself with the pattern, and one sheet of paper is easier to take to the loom.

Chart 192, Magenta with Dark Fuchsia on Natural.

—Chart Nos.—
1, 2, 3, 4

— Chart Nos.—
5, 6, 7, 8

—Chart Nos.—
9, 10, 11, 12

— Chart Nos.—
13, 14, 15, 16

—Chart Nos.—
17, 18, 19, 20

— *Chart Nos.*—
21, 22, 23, 24

—Chart Nos.—
25, 26, 27, 28

— Chart Nos. —
29, 30, 31, 32

—Chart Nos.—
33, 34, 35, 36

— Chart Nos.—
37, 38, 39, 40

— Chart Nos. —
41, 42, 43, 44

— Chart Nos.—
45, 46, 47, 48

— Chart Nos. —
49, 50, 51, 52

— Chart Nos. —
53, 54, 55, 56

— Chart Nos. —
57, 58, 59, 60

— Chart Nos.—
61, 62, 63, 64

—Chart Nos.—
65, 66, 67, 68

—Chart Nos.—
69, 70, 71, 72

—Chart Nos.—
73, 74, 75, 76

—Chart Nos.—
77, 78, 79, 80

— Chart Nos.—
81, 82, 83, 84

— Chart Nos.—
85, 86, 87, 88

— Chart Nos. —
89, 90, 91, 92

— Chart Nos.—
93, 94, 95, 96

—*Chart Nos.*—
97, 98, 99, 100

— Chart Nos.—
101, 102, 103, 104

— Chart Nos.—
105, 106, 107, 108

— Chart Nos. —
109, 110, 111, 112

—Chart Nos.—
113, 114, 115, 116

— Chart Nos.—
117, 118, 119, 120

— Chart Nos. —
121, 122, 123, 124

—Chart Nos.—
125, 126, 127, 128

— Chart Nos.—
129, 130, 131, 132

— Chart Nos.—
133, 134, 135, 136

— Chart Nos. —
137, 138, 139, 140

— Chart Nos. —
145, 146, 147, 148

—Chart Nos.—
149, 150, 151, 152

—Chart Nos.—
153, 154, 155, 156

—Chart Nos.—
161, 162, 163, 164

— Chart Nos.—
165, 166, 167, 168

— Chart Nos.—
169, 170, 171, 172

— Chart Nos.—
173, 174, 175, 176

— Chart Nos.—
177, 178, 179, 180

— *Chart Nos.—*
181, 182, 183, 184

— Chart Nos.—
185, 186, 187, 188

— Chart Nos.—
189, 190, 191, 192

— Chart Nos. —
193, 194, 195, 196

— Chart Nos.—
197, 198, 199, 200

— Chart Nos.—
201, 202, 203, 204

— *Chart Nos.*—
205, 206, 207, 208

— Chart Nos. —
209, 210, 211, 212

—Chart Nos.—
213, 214, 215, 216

— Chart Nos.—
217, 218, 219, 220

— Chart Nos.—
221, 222, 223, 224

—Chart Nos.—
225, 226, 227, 228

— Chart Nos.—
229, 230, 231, 232

— Chart Nos. —
233, 234, 235, 236

— *Chart Nos.*—
237, 238, 239, 240

— Chart Nos. —
241, 242, 243, 244

— Chart Nos.—
245, 246, 247, 248

— *Chart Nos.* —
249, 250, 251, 252

— Chart Nos.—
253, 254, 255, 256

—Chart Nos.—
257, 258, 259, 260

—*Chart Nos.*—
261, 262, 263, 264

— Chart Nos.—
265, 266, 267, 268

— Chart Nos.—
269, 270, 271, 272

— Chart Nos.—
273, 274, 275, 276

— Chart Nos.—
277, 278, 279, 280

— *Chart Nos.* —
281, 282, 283, 284

— Chart Nos. —
285, 286, 287, 288

Transitions

The patterns in this book all have 13 pattern ends, so you can combine any of them in the same band. Some options for charting smooth transitions are shown in fig. 5. From left to right:

Example 1

These motifs from Charts 143 and 147 were easily combined with no adjustments necessary. All of the motifs from Charts 141 to 200 have the same chevron-shaped outlines and could be used in the same way.

Example 2

These motifs from Charts 25 and 57 have different outlines, but they still partially dovetail together. A smooth transition was easily created with an arrangement of flecks between them.

Example 3

These motifs from Charts 37 and 65 have different outlines and don't dovetail together, but a smooth transition can always be created with an arrangement of flecks that fits the space.

Example 4

Here's another option for combining the motifs from example 3. A diagonal cross between each motif effectively frames the motifs, forming a distinct separation.

Charting Transitions

The design conventions for this pick-up technique are illustrated by all the charts in this book. Notice that in any vertical column, both blank squares and dark squares span one, three, or five rows, and flecks or floats in adjacent columns are offset by one row, thus forming stairstepped diagonal design lines. (At the beginning of the charts, you see spans of two and four blank squares because the design has been clipped horizontally. Fig. 3 shows how these areas look when woven.)

Design Tips

If you're combining different motifs, rather than repeating one over and over, consider their relative sizes and styles. Will they make a harmonious combination? The motifs in example 1 share the same outline, and the motifs in example 2 share the same main pattern element, but in each case the clear difference in size creates a pleasing division of space. In examples 3 and 4, the lines of flecks in one motif echo the lines of flecks in the other, while the variations in shape provide visual interest. To create continuity through repetition, I like to use the same separator motif or the same style of background elements at each transition in a band.

Fig. 5: These motifs from different charts have been combined with one another, using separator motifs or arrangements of flecks to make graceful transitions.

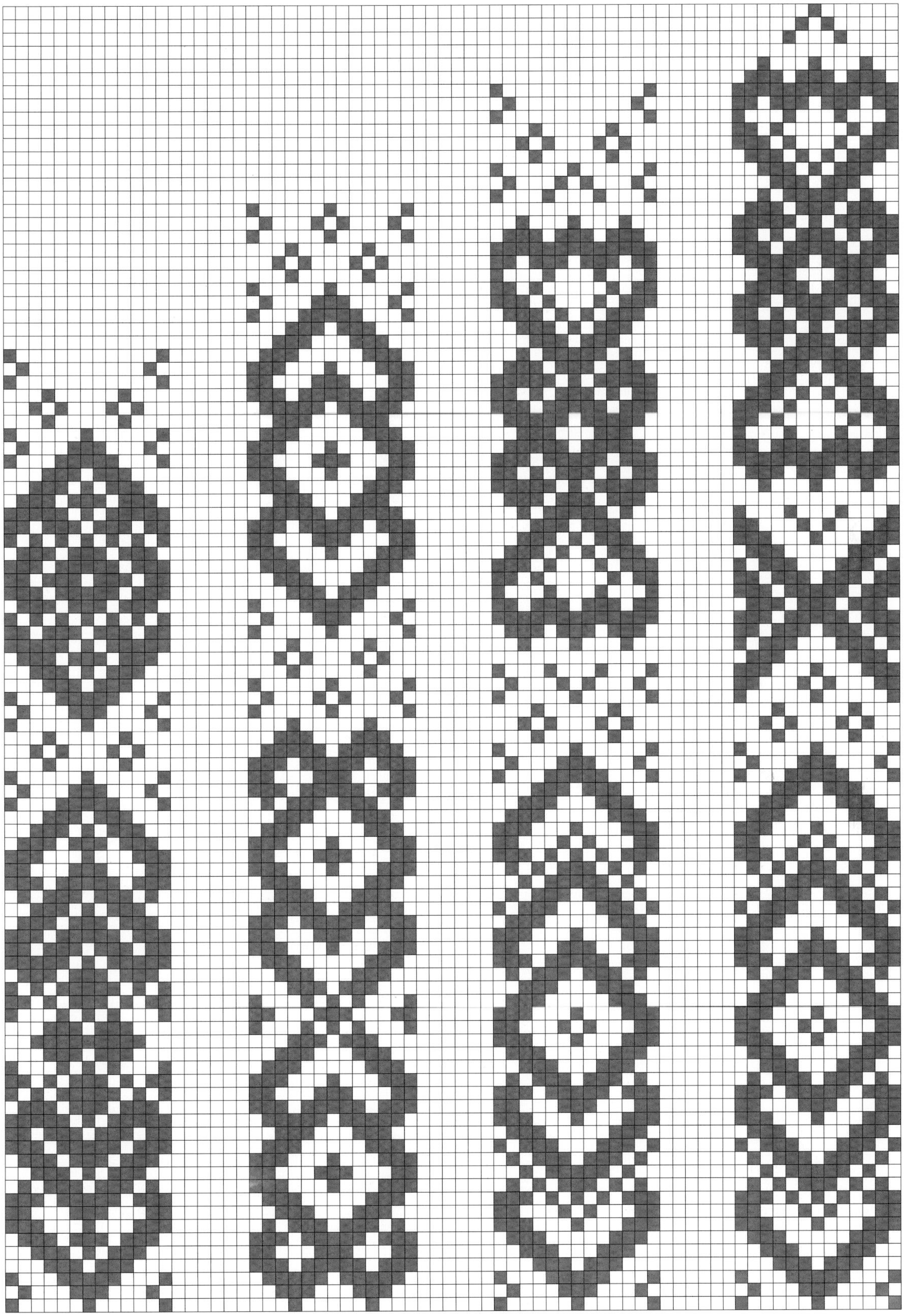

My Design Process

The first pick-up pattern I wove many years ago was taken from a photo of a Finnish ski belt in *Byways in Handweaving* (Atwater 1954, 32). A hatched diamond motif from that band formed the beginning of the collection in this book. I increased the number of pattern ends from 11 to 13, connected multiple diamonds end to end (Chart 1), and came up with different ways to fill the inside space (Charts 2–12).

My first designs were developed from the same classic motif. I added straight and hooked diagonals extending from the outside, erased parts of the hatched diamond to create a heart, combined diamonds and hearts, and added chevrons, diagonal crosses, and arrangements of flecks as frames and separators. Then I began varying the motifs in dozens of other ways, including enlarging the diamonds to open up more possibilities for patterning inside them. Each chart I drew sparked new ideas. Some were tossed, others were refined and saved, and over time my collection grew.

I love the process of sketching pick-up patterns with pencil and graph paper. I'm fascinated not only by the visual appeal of the motifs but also by how they develop from the staggered threading as an integral part of the weave structure itself. This connection of the motifs to the weave structure gives me a comfortable framework for my creativity.

To preserve this connection, I don't use straight horizontal design lines as I sketch. I limit myself to patterns that always stay in sync with the staggered threading and form diagonal design lines, with floats over three or five shots, never two or four. I like such patterns because designing and weaving them feels rhythmic and intuitive to me and because all the design elements dovetail gracefully together.

As I evaluate each design, I consider both the dark and light areas. The reverse side of a band—where the raised pattern and textured background change places in the design—can be as pleasing as the face. Because I'm intrigued by this concept, I designed some simple patterns that show the positive/negative effect on the same side (Charts 233–252). That led me to design a similar kind of notched frame for encasing diamond motifs (Charts 201–220) and to sketch seamless light/dark reversals with larger, more intricate motifs (Charts 221–232). These notched frames provide a way to create design lines that appear horizontal while still staying in sync with the staggered threading.

I've been enriched and inspired by the Scandinavian traditions of this heritage craft, and I gratefully acknowledge this influence. My own design process consists simply of sketching and erasing arrangements of flecks and floats, over and over, until I'm pleased with what emerges. Since these patterns are a natural outgrowth of the weave structure itself, the pattern elements that form as I sketch are part of the universal language of this technique. I enjoy using this language to create new variations, and I hope you find much in these pages to inspire your own work.

How a Pattern Takes Shape

Each pattern evolves in a different way, but the last 16 charts in this collection illustrate some examples.

For **Chart 273,** I connected two diamond motifs from **Chart 152** and noticed that an interesting cross-and-heart shape formed at the intersection. For **Chart 274,** I used the cross-and-heart as a separator between the diamonds, and for **Charts 275** and **276,** I used it as the main element to design two new patterns.

For **Chart 277,** I connected cross-and-heart motifs to make a continuous pattern. For **Chart 278,** I isolated part of the continuous pattern to form a diamond motif, and for **Charts 279** and **280,** I modified that diamond to create two larger ones.

For **Charts 281–288,** I began with the cross-and-heart, expanded it lengthwise in the center, then varied the design to create eight new motifs of various sizes and configurations.

You can see how this process could easily continue. There are always so many possibilities.

Fig. 6: Graph paper with eight squares to the inch, a pencil, eraser, and eraser shield are basic supplies for charting patterns. A scrap of unbleached muslin is handy for cleaning the eraser, and a ruler helps outline the number of columns needed. For designing, a no. 2 (HB) pencil is good for lightly sketching in floats and flecks because it can be erased cleanly to make changes. A soft black drawing pencil with a thick lead (6B, 7B, or 8B) is hard to erase cleanly but makes it easy to darken a lighter sketch to finalize a design or make a new copy.

Chart 175, Cobalt Blue with Dark Sierra on Natural and Paradise.

Part 2

Color in Pick-Up

Color in Pick-Up

As intriguing as patterns are, color is what brings them alive and gives them personality. In bright hues on a black or white background, a pattern might pop with excitement, while in a subtle tone-on-tone combination, it might radiate a quiet richness. There's something truly satisfying about seeing an eye-catching motif come to life in colors that please you.

In this section of the book, we'll focus only on the pattern area of the band—on ways to arrange colors with the pattern warp, background warp, and weft. Borders can be added to frame the design with additional colors, but they're not dealt with here.

My approach to color within the pattern area is simple: I want to keep the focus on the motifs, and I don't want them to be broken up with a too-busy color arrangement. If I think of the motifs as characters in a story and the colors as their clothes, I want the motifs to wear the colors and not the other way around.

Before we look at some of the ways that colors can be arranged in a pick-up band, let's look at the characteristics that differentiate individual colors from one another.

Color Characteristics

Colors can vary from one another in hue, intensity, and value. If one yarn color doesn't feel quite right when you place it with another to preview a combination, try exchanging it for one with slightly different characteristics. For example, if a green color comes on too strongly, you might consider a lighter, darker, or more muted version of the same hue. If it isn't harmonizing well, ask yourself if a green that leans toward blue or yellow would be more pleasing with the other colors you've chosen. Color decisions are personal choices—unique to each weaver—and you'll intuitively know when you have it right for you.

Hue refers to the color itself—a red hue, an orange hue, and so forth. Color wheels, like the one I've approximated with perle cotton in fig. 7, are often divided into 12 pure hues, each of which acts as a representative for the many variations within its family. Both scarlet and crimson are hues in the red family, for example, but scarlet leans more toward orange and crimson leans more toward violet.

Intensity refers to the purity of a color. Hues can range from bright and clear, to duller and more muted. Kelly is a bright green, for example, and moss is a more muted one.

Value refers to how light or dark a color is. Sky is a light value of blue, for example, and navy is a dark one. Pure hues aren't all the same value—yellow is the lightest and violet is the darkest.

The Importance of Value

Value is the most important characteristic when it comes to how the eye reads the pattern in a band. The more value contrast there is between the background and pattern colors, the more clearly the motifs will stand out. With a big value difference, the pattern will pop with lots of visual punch. With less value difference, the effect is more muted. With no value difference, it can be hard to see the pattern clearly, and that can be disappointing if it isn't what you had in mind.

Fig. 7: Finger hanks of perle cotton, arranged to approximate a color wheel. Some of the available colors for this brand of yarn don't exactly match the pure hues you'd see on an artist's color wheel, but that's okay for our purposes. Each little hank is simply a placeholder for the many variations within its hue family, and together they form a visual reference for thinking about how colors relate to one another.

Fig. 8: The light green in the tiny sample doesn't have much punch on the natural background, but that might be just what you want. As an accent to the dark green in the leftmost sample, the light green adds an effective, subtle glow, and as a background color in the center sample, it adds a layer of interest. The red samples illustrate how the same motif looks different with different background colors.

Chart 61, Winter Green with Bali on Natural.
Chart 147, Bali on Natural.
Charts 149–152, Winter Green on Yellow and Bali.
Chart 149, Red on Natural; Red on Yellow and Light Orange.

About the Sample Bands

Throughout this section, you'll find dozens of woven samples that illustrate various color arrangements. Most are fringed at one end and hemmed at the other. The capitalized color names in the captions are those assigned by Supreme, the manufacturer of the perle cotton I used—size 3/2 for the pattern and 5/2 for the background and weft. For point of reference, the samples are all about ¹⁵⁄₁₆" wide. See page 120 for the warp drafts.

Fig. 9: Here the same purple pattern color is woven in three arrangements—with an accent, in a tone-on-tone combination, and with two background colors. The samples are folded to show both sides. The yarn wrap is a way to evaluate how the accent and main pattern color will look together before you warp the loom.

Chart 33, Purple with Light Rust on Natural.
Chart 54, Purple on Grotto.
Chart 200, Purple on Natural and Quince.

Weft Color Choices

Little skips of weft are visible inside and around motifs wherever pattern ends have been suppressed and not allowed to form tabby flecks. The weft color often matches the background, but a lighter weft color can create a delicate beaded look. I like the pleasing sparks of light that white weft skips add to a colored background, as in the middle sample in fig. 9. I don't use colored weft on a white background because, to my eye, it muddies the look instead of enhancing it.

Background Color

Single background color. Pick-up patterns are by nature visually striking, and since there's a lot going on patternwise within the space of a narrow band, there doesn't need to be a lot going on colorwise. Simple pairings of one background color with one pattern color can be an effective way to present any design.

Light or dark. I think of background colors as supporting players that will step back to let the pattern colors stand out. I like natural white for the background of most bands because it creates a feeling of clarity and spaciousness, gives the eye a place to rest, and makes it easy to see the appealing basketweave texture in the background. See fig. 13. A dark background creates a different look, and black is a classic choice that works with any lighter pattern color. See fig. 21.

Two background colors. Using two background colors is an interesting way to introduce more color. I usually use natural white for one and a light color for the other and let the skips of white weft tie the two together. Often the light color can evoke the same feeling as a subtle wash of watercolor or glaze would in another medium. Placing the white on the sides creates one look, and placing it in the middle creates another, as illustrated by pairs of samples in figs. 10, 15, and 17.

Tone-on-tone combinations. To create a tone-on-tone design, I use a light color for the background and a darker value of the same or similar hue for the pattern. Then, since there's relatively little contrast between background and pattern, I use natural white weft to add a spark of light and accentuate the shapes of the motifs. See fig. 18 and the middle sample in fig. 9.

More Than One Pattern Color

Accents. Pattern ends that contrast with the main pattern color in hue, intensity, or value can emphasize pivot points and add visual interest. Placing three ends in the center, as in the leftmost sample in fig. 9, works well for most combinations. If there's a lot of value contrast, consider an accent of one end in the center instead. An accent from a hue family that is opposite or nearly opposite on the color wheel can liven up a design. An accent from a hue family that is adjacent on the color

Fig. 10: The only difference between these two samples is the placement of the background colors.

Chart 173, Dark Sierra with Burnt Orange on Natural and Melon.

Fig. 11: Wraps of the pattern colors and twists of the background/pattern pairs, like these for the bands in fig. 12, can help you visualize color interactions before you warp the loom.

Fig. 12: Placing five ends of one pattern color in the center can be especially effective with two background colors. These samples are folded to show both sides.

Chart 98, Light Rust and Dark Sierra on Daffodil and Pistachio. Chart 277, Light Rust and Evergreen on Natural and Pistachio.

wheel can enhance a design in a more subtle way. A bright accent can seem to glow when paired with a muted or dark color from the same or adjacent hue family.

Same value pairs. If two dark pattern colors have the same value, the eye will read the pattern as a unified whole even if the hues are completely unrelated, and such pairings can bring a subtle complexity to a design. One color can be used in the center only, as in fig. 6, or the two colors can be alternated without creating distracting stripes—two of one, three of another, and so forth—as in fig. 14.

Gradations. Three pattern colors of the same hue that form a subtle gradation from darker to lighter add depth to the motifs. The color ranges of many weaving yarns don't include such gradations, but you can also look for adjacent hues that naturally form a gradation in value, as in fig. 19. Since gradations already involve some change in value, colors that are closely related—in both hue and intensity—keep the motifs from being broken up by stripes.

Five in the center. The samples in fig. 12 have five ends of one pattern color in the center and two background colors. Whereas three ends in the center creates an accent, five in the center creates a more dominant area of color. I like to make the five ends the darker of the two pattern colors and place them against the darker background. Depending on the relative hues and values of the colors and their placement, this arrangement can form a smooth blend, as with the brown, or it can create lines that emphasize the center sections of the motifs, as with the green.

Characteristics in common. When you look at a band with more than one pattern color, notice what the pattern colors have in common with one another. An accent that contrasts in hue with the main pattern color might be similar in value and intensity. An accent from a neighboring hue family might differ in value and

intensity but be closely related in hue. Gradations differ in value but are related in hue. Differences provide interest and similarities create unity.

Fig. 13: The rust pattern color works well on its own or as an accent to contrasting hues of green or blue.

Chart 45, Dark Turq with Burnt Orange on Natural.
Chart 134, Evergreen with Burnt Orange on Natural.
Chart 141, Burnt Orange on Natural.

Testing Color Arrangements

Twists for background/pattern combinations. To test the value contrast between the background and pattern yarns, make a twisted cord or simply twirl the strands together in your hand. Hold the twist at arm's length and squint to get a better perspective, or view it with the monochrome setting on a camera to remove the hues and show only the values. The more distinct a barber pole you see, the more the motifs will stand out from the background.

Wraps for multiple pattern colors. Yarn wraps of the pattern colors show how they'll look side by side before you warp the loom. View them as described for twists, above. Beware of extreme value differences, since marked stripes can break up the motifs. For same-value pairs, look for hues that appear the same shade of gray in monochrome. For gradations, look for values that almost melt into one another so the eye can travel smoothly across the pattern without stopping.

Wraps and twists, like those in fig. 11, and charts drawn with colored pencils, like those in fig. 13, can help you evaluate designs ahead of time, but the effects can't be fully appreciated until pattern and color come together on the loom. There's always an element of surprise, and that's part of the fun.

Practical Examples of Color Combinations

In figs. 14–23 on the following pages, you'll find dozens of woven samples that illustrate a variety of ways to arrange color in pick-up bands.

Fig. 14a. Same-value pair: Here alternating pattern colors bring a subtle complexity to the design. The blue and brown are the same value, so the motifs are not broken up by stripes even though the hues are completely unrelated. The natural white weft lightens the gold background and accentuates the diagonal design lines.

Chart 95, Cobalt Blue and Dark Sierra on California Gold.

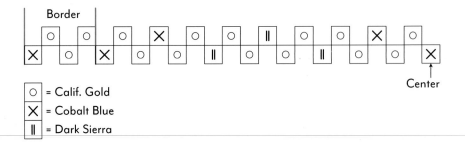

○ = Calif. Gold
✕ = Cobalt Blue
‖ = Dark Sierra

Fig. 14b. Detail: The skips of white weft against the gold background add pleasing sparks of light that liven up this design.

Fig. 15a. Contrasting hues: Colors from hue families that are opposite on the color wheel have nothing in common, but in the right proportions they complement one another beautifully. Bright blue and orange would create quite an intense combination, so my preference is for dark or muted versions of these hues.

Chart 90, Light Rust on Natural.
Chart 67, Cobalt Blue with Light Rust on Natural.
Chart 147, Cobalt Blue on Natural.
Chart 106, Cobalt Blue with Burnt Orange on Natural and California Gold.
Chart 191, Cobalt Blue with Burnt Orange on California Gold and Natural.

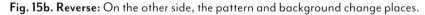

Fig. 15b. Reverse: On the other side, the pattern and background change places.

Fig. 16a. Dark neutrals: Black or brown on natural white has a classic appeal. Black makes a stronger impact because of the sharper value contrast between the pattern and background colors, whereas brown creates a slightly softer impression. Dark neutrals like these work well on their own and are easy to combine with other colors in the background.

Chart 114, Black on Natural.
Chart 40, Black on Natural and Light Rust.
Chart 119, Dark Sierra on Natural.
Chart 154, Dark Sierra on Natural and Pistachio.
Chart 156, Dark Sierra on Natural and Tyrol.

Fig. 16b. Reverse: On the other side, the pattern and background change places.

Fig. 17a. Accents of related vs. contrasting hues: When dark red is paired with brown—a color from a neighboring hue family—the combination has an understated richness. When the same dark red is paired with dark green—a color from a hue family that is opposite on the color wheel—the combination has a more lively feel.

Chart 161 and Chart 162, Lipstick with Dark Sierra on Natural and California Gold.
Chart 126, Evergreen with Lipstick on Natural and California Gold.
Chart 284, Lipstick with Dark Sierra on California Gold and Natural.
Chart 82, Lipstick on Natural.
Chart 277, Evergreen with Lipstick on California Gold and Natural.

Fig. 17b. Reverse: On the other side, the pattern and background change places.

Fig. 18a. Tone-on-tone combinations: These samples were woven with a light color for the background and a darker value of the same or similar hue for the pattern. The natural white weft lightens the background and accentuates the motifs. Patterns in such combinations have a quiet, understated appeal.

Chart 97, Jade Green on Teal.
Chart 17, Old Gold on Champagne.
Chart 129, Evergreen on Scarab.
Chart 92, Dark Sierra on Light Rust.
Chart 136, Soldier Blue on Periwinkle.
Chart 103, Burnt Orange on Melon.
Chart 39, Dark Green on Duck.

Fig. 18b. Reverse: On the other side, the pattern and background change places.

Fig. 19a. Pattern color gradation: Here three values form a gradation from dark at the sides to light in the middle. To avoid marked stripes, look for a subtle range of values that blend smoothly into one another, either in closely related hues—as with these samples—or in one hue if the color range of the yarn you're using includes value gradations.

Chart 69, Magenta, Red, and Tangerine on Natural.
Chart 21 (modified), Red, Tangerine, and Light Orange on Natural.

Fig. 19b. Modified pattern color gradation: The lightest of the three blue-green colors was too light to create a smooth gradation with the others (see the yarn wrap at the top), so I limited it to one pattern end in the center of the band (see the yarn wrap at the bottom). This lessened its impact and added spark to the design without creating a marked stripe.

Charts 163 and 164, Forest Green, Jade Green, and Teal on Natural.

Fig. 20a. Combining related hues: Colors from the same or neighboring hue families are easy to combine because they have so much in common. Here magenta is paired with a light, dusty orange in the background, and dark green is paired with blue-greens that are lighter and brighter and add a subtle glow—one as an accent and one as a second background color.

Chart 178, Magenta on Natural and Melon.
Chart 30, Dark Green on Natural.
Chart 89, Dark Green with Jade Green on Natural.
Chart 36, Magenta on Natural.
Chart 186, Dark Green on Natural and Crab.

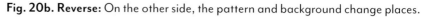

Fig. 20b. Reverse: On the other side, the pattern and background change places.

Fig. 21a. Dark backgrounds: Black is a classic choice for a dark background and works well with any lighter pattern color, but there are also lots of other possibilities.

Chart 105, Gold on Burnt Orange.
Chart 166, Burnt Orange on Black.
Chart 112, Old Gold on Black.
Chart 72, Light Rust on Black.
Chart 108, Gold on Cobalt Blue.

Fig. 21b. Reverse: On the other side, the pattern and background change places.

Fig. 22a. Subtle shift in background colors: This band has three background colors, with a pale, creamy yellow placed between the gold on the sides and the natural white in the middle to soften the dividing line. The warp draft shows how I modified a warp draft for two background colors to add a third.

Chart 288, Black on California Gold, Champagne, and Natural.

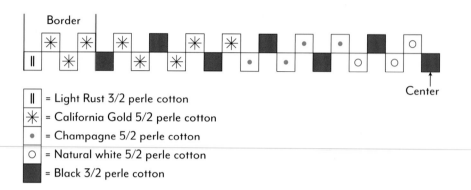

| = Light Rust 3/2 perle cotton
✳ = California Gold 5/2 perle cotton
• = Champagne 5/2 perle cotton
○ = Natural white 5/2 perle cotton
■ = Black 3/2 perle cotton

Fig. 22b. Detail: Placing the pale yellow between the gold and white softens the shift in background colors and creates a blended effect.

Fig. 23a. Single pattern color on white: A simple color arrangement like this—of a medium or dark color on natural white—is an effective way to present any design.

Chart 220, Dark Green on Natural.
Chart 218, Magenta on Natural.
Chart 219, Dark Green on Natural.
Chart 217, Special Turq on Natural.

Fig. 23b. Reverse: On the other side, the pattern and background change places.

Fig. 24: In these samples, alternating light/dark reversals create interesting checked designs.

Chart 242, Special Turq on Natural.
Chart 243, Dark Green on Natural.
Chart 252, Magenta on Natural.
Chart 240, Special Turq on Natural.
Chart 249, Magenta on Natural.
Chart 251, Special Turq on Natural.

Key to Woven Samples by Chart Number

Fig. 25: This pattern is a seamless light/dark reversal—like those in fig. 24 but with a larger, more intricate motif.

Chart 221, Dark Green on Natural.

Yarn Choices and Warp Drafts

For this pick-up technique, the pattern ends should be thicker than the background ends and weft. The samples in this book were woven with Supreme perle cotton—size 3/2 for the pattern and 5/2 for the background and weft. Size 5/2 doubled for the pattern would yield similar results.

See figs. 14 and 22 for the warp drafts used for those bands. On these two pages are the rest of the warp drafts that I used for the woven samples.

Each draft has 13 pattern ends and 45 ends total. Read from left to right through the center, then from right to left. The two rows represent the two threading positions on the loom—open/heddle on an inkle loom, hole/slot on a band heddle, and odd/even shafts on a floor or table loom.

On the pattern heddle—Norwegian *spaltegrind* or Swedish *mönsterbandgrind*, a hole-and-slot heddle with dedicated short slots for the pattern ends—the pattern ends are threaded in the special slots, and the background and border ends are threaded in the regular holes and slots.

The ends in pattern color in the borders aren't treated as pattern ends. They're placed at the selvedges so the weft turns, which are in a contrasting color, will create a whipstitched effect around them. You can of course replace these simple borders with those of your own design in any width and color sequence.

Single Pattern Color

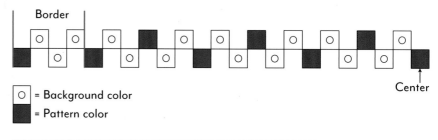

O = Background color

■ = Pattern color

Accent

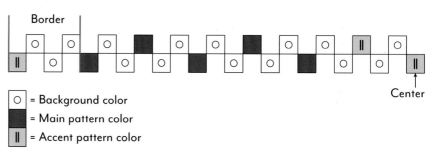

O = Background color

■ = Main pattern color

‖ = Accent pattern color

Two Background Colors

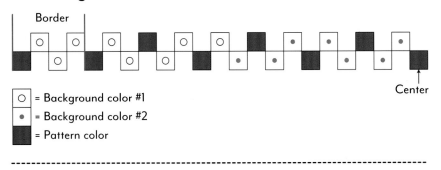

○	= Background color #1
•	= Background color #2
■	= Pattern color

Accent of Three with Two Background Colors

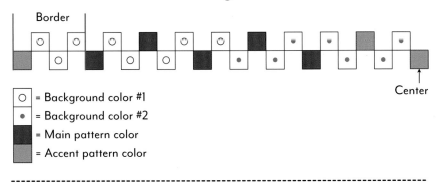

○	= Background color #1
•	= Background color #2
■	= Main pattern color
▨	= Accent pattern color

Five in the Center with Two Background Colors

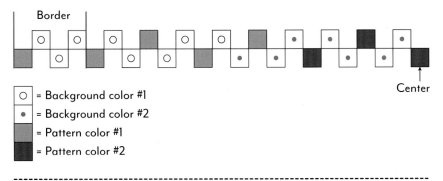

○	= Background color #1
•	= Background color #2
▨	= Pattern color #1
■	= Pattern color #2

Gradation

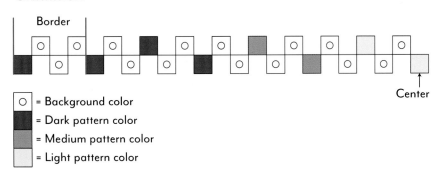

○	= Background color
■	= Dark pattern color
▨	= Medium pattern color
▢	= Light pattern color

Fig. 26: I use the term "diamond" for any motif that begins and ends with opposing chevrons, even if they are not connected at the sides, as in this example.

Chart 154, Dark Sierra on Natural and Pistachio.

Acknowledgments

I'm grateful to my wonderfully supportive editor, Sandra Korinchak, and the whole talented team at Schiffer for making this book possible.

I'm grateful to Mary Skoy for proofreading my manuscript and to my brother, Boyd Carson, for the conversations we had about family and creativity.

And I'm grateful to my friends and fellow weavers, who supported me in so many ways:

Lorraine Hosler, Shelley Peters, Bonnie Schuster, Karla Long, and Barbara Hand were always there with thoughtful comments and encouragement.

Mary Skoy, Susan Kolstad, Jan Mostrom, Solveig Pollei, Jan Kroyer, and Wendy Sundquist backed me up with the wisdom and moral support of the Posse.

Thank you all.

Fig. 27: Patterns are drawn on a square grid but appear more elongated when woven.

Chart 156, Dark Sierra on Natural and Tyrol.

Glossary

accent—The visual emphasis created by certain pattern ends—usually one or three in the center—that contrast with the others in hue, intensity, or value.

background area—An area of texture in background color inside or around a motif. See *basketweave texture.*

background elements—Small motifs or arrangements of flecks in pattern color that decorate background areas and form transitions between motifs.

background end—An end in background color. Background ends are not manipulated to form the pattern.

band heddle—A small hole-and-slot heddle used for bandweaving, usually in a backstrap arrangement.

basketweave texture—The interlacement that forms in background areas wherever a pattern end that would have normally formed a tabby fleck on that shot has been suppressed (if weaving on the band heddle or inkle loom) or not selected (if weaving on the pattern heddle). At these points, a skip or tiny span of weft shows on the face, and two background ends lie side by side under the skip.

chart—A representation of a pick-up pattern on graph paper. Each vertical column represents one pattern end and each horizontal row represents one shot of weft. Background ends are not represented.

chevron—A V- or inverted V-shaped motif.

column—A vertical line of squares in a chart.

cross—A diagonal cross or X-shaped motif.

diagonals—Slanting design lines in the pattern, composed of floats or flecks on adjacent pattern ends.

diamond—A diamond-shaped motif. I use the term for any motif that begins and ends with opposing chevrons even if they are not connected at the sides.

element—A component of the pattern, such as a fleck, float, motif, background area, or background element.

end—A single warp thread.

face—The side of the band that faces the weaver when the band is on the loom.

fleck—The spot of color that a pattern end naturally forms on alternate shots when a staggered threading is woven in warp-faced tabby. Some flecks are used as elements in patterns, and others are suppressed (if weaving on the band heddle or inkle loom) or not selected (if weaving on the pattern heddle) to form background areas.

float—The pattern element that is created when a pattern end is present on the face for three or five consecutive shots.

gradation—A group of colors, usually of the same hue, that form a subtle range in value from darker to lighter.

heart—A stylized heart-shaped motif.

inkle loom—A small loom for bandweaving that consists of pegs set into a frame. It has fixed heddles and a device, often a sliding peg, to tension the warp.

hue—Refers to the color itself. For example, scarlet and cardinal are red hues.

intensity—Refers to the purity of a color. For example, a bright kelly green is a purer, more intense hue than a muted moss green.

motif—A shape formed by an arrangement of floats and flecks on adjacent pattern ends. A compound motif can consist of several motifs that are closely spaced and designed so they are viewed as a single unit.

notched frame—I use this term for a motif with a notched outline, like a crenellated wall, as in Charts 233–252, which can be expanded to frame another motif, as in Charts 201–232.

pattern—The overall design in a pick-up-woven band, which is composed of motifs, background areas, and background elements.

pattern end—An end in pattern color. For this type of pick-up bandweaving, the pattern ends are thicker than the background ends.

pattern heddle—A type of band heddle with special short slots for the pattern ends. This causes the pattern ends to float in the middle of each shed, where they can be selected to form the pattern.

pick-up bandweaving—A system of weaving in which patterns are formed by hand manipulation of the warp as a band is being woven. There are different types of pick-up bandweaving, each of which begins with a specific threading, follows certain conventions, and results in a distinctive pattern style. The type that is the subject of this book is referred to by many weavers as Baltic style. It is based on a staggered threading and naturally produces geometric patterns based on diagonal design lines.

reverse—The side of the band that does not face the weaver when the band is on the loom.

row—One horizontal line of squares in a warp draft or pattern chart.

separator—A smaller motif used to separate the main motifs in a pattern.

shed—The space between warp ends through which the weft is passed. Two sheds are required for this pick-up technique. See *tabby.*

shot—One pass of the weft through a shed. A more commonly used term for shot is pick, but I do not use it in connection with bandweaving in order to avoid confusion with terms for pick-up weaving.

skip—See *basketweave texture.*

staggered threading—The threading used for this type of pick-up bandweaving, in which the thicker pattern ends are always separated by two background ends. When woven in warp-faced tabby, the threading produces alternating flecks in pattern color.

tabby—A system of interlacement with a two-shot sequence in which the weft travels over and under alternate warp ends on one shot and over and under the opposite warp ends on the next shot. A synonym for tabby is plain weave, but according to Dorothy K. Burnham, plain weave has an imprecise meaning, and "tabby is recommended as a more specific term." (Burnham 1981, 101) The bands in this book are woven in pick-up on a foundation of warp-faced tabby.

threading—A plan for a warp. See *warp draft.*

transition—The arrangement of elements where the pattern changes from one motif to the next or between tabby and pick-up.

value—Refers to the lightness or darkness of a color. For example, sky is a light value of blue and navy is a dark value.

warp—The lengthwise threads in a woven textile that are interlaced at right angles with the weft.

warp draft—A notation on graph paper showing the threading for a specific band. It specifies the order of colors and shows the two alternating threading positions that produce tabby on the loom.

warp-faced—Describes a textile in which a closely spaced warp covers the weft.

warp-faced tabby band—A warp-faced band woven in tabby with no pick-up.

weave structure—A system of interlacement, such as tabby, used to form a textile.

weft—The crosswise thread in a woven textile that is interlaced at right angles with the warp.

References

Atwater, Mary Meigs. *Byways in Handweaving.* New York: Macmillan, 1954.

Burnham, Dorothy K. *Warp and Weft, a Dictionary of Textile Terms.* Toronto: Royal Ontario Museum, 1980. US edition, New York: Charles Scribner's Sons, 1981.

Torgenrud, Heather. *Norwegian Pick-Up Bandweaving.* Atglen, PA: Schiffer, 2014.

Trotzig, Liv, and Astrid Axelsson. *Band.* Västerås, Sweden: ICA-förlaget, 1972.

Further Reading

Books with patterns and instructions in this pick-up technique:

Dixon, Anne. *Weaver's Inkle Pattern Directory.* Loveland, CO: Interweave, 2012.

Foulkes, Susan. *Weaving Patterned Bands.* Atglen, PA: Schiffer, 2018.

Torgenrud, Heather. *Norwegian Pick-Up Bandweaving.* Atglen, PA: Schiffer, 2014.

Fig. 28: When woven in warp-faced tabby, the staggered threading for this pick-up technique produces alternating flecks in pattern color, as you can see above the fringe in the sample at right.

Charts 143 and 88, Cobalt Blue with Burnt Orange on California Gold and Natural.

Susan M. Kolstad

Heather Torgenrud studied traditional weaving in Norway and Sweden, and teaches pick-up techniques and bandweaving, including at the Vesterheim Norwegian-American Museum. Her articles and patterns have appeared in publications such as *Handwoven* and the *Norwegian Textile Letter*. Heather originally taught herself to weave on a table loom. In 1972, the gift of an inkle loom sparked a fascination with pick-up. After spending time studying and documenting museum bands, she combined her passion for traditional bands and her practical approach to color to focus on pattern design. She is also the author of *Norwegian Pick-Up Bandweaving*. Visit her at norwegianpickupbandweaving.com.